D0548008

This book belongs to

....

Five-minute
FARMYARD
— Tales —

p

CONTENTS

— Old —
EVEREST

Everest was one of the biggest horses in the world. He was also one of the strongest. When he was young, and already twice as big as other horses, he pulled the heavy cart filled with peas or potatoes, cabbages or corn, and everything grown on the farm. He took the vegetables from the farm down to the market, and he brought things from the market back to the farm. He pulled the huge machine that cut the wheat to make flour. He pulled the big plough that dug the soil, so the farmer could plant the seed that grew into wheat that made the flour...

...that Everest took to market. He did everything!

Everest was the best...but that was ages ago.

"So why don't you do everything now?" asked Puff the Pig.

"The farmer thinks I'm too old," said Everest, sadly. "He is only trying to be kind. He thinks I need a rest."

Jacob the Lamb said, "I bet you are still stronger than anything, Everest! Nothing is as strong as you!" The huge horse lowered his head.

"Well...I am not as strong as I was, little one," smiled Everest. "Anyway, farms don't use horses any more. The farmer uses a tractor instead!"

The big old horse had lots of time to think about when he was young and still worked on the farm. He spent most of the time now in his favourite meadow nibbling grass, and, when he grew bored with that, chasing rabbits or chickens, or biting large chunks out of the hedge. But if Parsnip the Sheep, Waddle the Goose, or Scratchitt the Cat were in his field, he would tell them his stories. Sometimes he told the same stories again without realising, but no one really minded.

But Everest still thought about the tractor. It wasn't the tractor's fault. He just wanted to work.

"Can this tractor pull the cart better than you?" asked Parsnip the Sheep.

"No," said Everest.

"Can the tractor pull the plough better than you?" asked Waddle the Goose.

"No," said Everest.

"Can the tractor cut the wheat better than you?" asked Scratchitt the Cat.

"No," said Everest.

"So why did the farmer buy the tractor?" Puff the Pig wanted to know. Everest lowered his huge head and sighed.

"He liked the colour," said Everest.

Then one day the farmer said to Everest, "I have a problem with that tractor of mine. It won't start! I would ask you to help, Everest, but I suppose you are enjoying your rest." Everest shook his head from side to side.

"Even so," said the farmer, "I need to plough the field and the plough won't fit a horse, just the tractor! I don't know what to do."

Everest nudged the farmer gently over to the barn where the tractor was kept. His reins and harness were there too. The puzzled farmer picked up an old rope and hooked it on the front of the tractor. Then, as easily as anything, Everest pulled the tractor out. Then he pulled the plough up behind the tractor.

"You mean you can pull both together?" said the farmer. Everest nodded his head up and down. The farmer was amazed! So the farmer hooked the plough to the tractor. Then he hooked the tractor to the horse. And Everest pulled the tractor and the tractor pulled the plough.

Together they ploughed the field in the fastest time ever.

Everest was still the biggest and the strongest... and now the happiest horse in the whole world.

— The —
CHICKLINGS

Duck and Hen both laid some eggs. They were very proud mothers. They would sit with silly smiles on their faces, fondly waiting for their eggs to hatch.

"Duck," said Hen, "let us put the eggs side by side, and see whose eggs are the most beautiful."

"If you like," said Duck, "but I already know mine are."

"Ha!" said Hen. "Wait until you have seen mine!"

Duck carried her eggs carefully, one by one, to a spot where there was soft hay on the ground. Hen carried her eggs over to the same spot and gently set them down beside Duck's. Duck picked up the first egg from her side.

"Look at this one! This egg is so smooth!" she said. They both looked at how smooth the egg was. Hen picked up an egg too.

"This one is smooth as well…and it is so round! Look at the lovely shape of this egg." They both looked at the shape of the egg. They put back those two eggs and picked up two others.

Duck said, "This one is smooth and shapely, and has beautiful freckles…"

By the time the last one was picked up and put back, the eggs were all mixed up together!

Hen said, "I am fatter than you, so my eggs must be the largest ones." So Duck picked out the smallest eggs and put them back in her nest. Hen picked out the largest eggs and took them back to hers. Then they sat on them until the eggs hatched and out popped fluffy ducklings and chicks.

One day Duck and Hen met with their babies.

"Now!" said Duck proudly. "Aren't these the handsomest ducklings you ever saw?"

"They are quite handsome," replied Hen, "but don't you think these are the most beautiful chicks in the whole world?"

"They are quite beautiful," replied Duck.

The next day, Duck taught her ducklings how to be ducklings.

"Walk behind me, one behind the other!" she told them. "We are going to the pond for swimming lessons." But the ducklings just couldn't walk one behind the other. They ran circles around Duck. They ran over her and under her, until Duck became quite dizzy watching them scoot about. When they reached the pond, the ducklings dipped their feet in the water, shook their heads and refused to go in.

Hen was teaching her chicks how to be chicks. She taught them to scratch and hop backwards to make the worms pop up out of the ground. But the chicks couldn't do it! They fell on their faces instead. She taught them to run all over the farm and look for their own food. They just followed her everywhere in a long line.

When Hen's back was turned, the chicks would cram into the dog's drinking bowl and would not come out! Josh the dog was lying next to his bowl. He opened one eye but didn't seem to mind. He would rather drink from the puddles anyway.

Duck and Hen sighed and sat down together to talk. They knew by now that they had each taken the wrong eggs. The ducklings were chicks, and the chicks were ducklings.

"Never mind," said Hen. "Let's just call them Chicklings, and we will always be right."

"One thing we have found out," said Duck. "is that the Chicklings are all beautiful. We would not have mixed them up, otherwise." Hen agreed, and they sat all afternoon, happily watching their chicklings play.

The ducklings played in the dog's bowl...

And the chicks played on the dog!

AUNTY
and the flowers

Every year on the farm, the animals had a competition. Everyone liked to join in the fun, and there was a prize for the winner. The prize could be for anything. One year, it was for growing the best purple vegetables. Once it was for having the knobbliest knees. (Gladys the duck won that, of course.) Once it was for the animal who could spell 'chrysanthemum'. The prize was not won at all that time…no one in the world can spell chrysanthemum! This year they decided the prize would be for the best display of flowers. But who would choose the winner? Most of the animals had already been judges in other years. Some of them had been judges more than once.

If Nelly the hen were the judge, she would make herself the winner. She always did.

Bramble the sheep caught her wool on everything. She pulled the tables and chairs down behind her wherever she went.

Blink the pig covered everything in mud.

Rambo the big horse couldn't even get into the tent!

But Aunty the goat wanted the job. She told the others how much she liked flowers. So why not? Aunty had never been a judge before and so she was chosen.

The big day came. Everyone had been busy for days. The tent was full of flowers, full of colour and light. There were no brown leaves on the flowers. There were no creepy-crawlies on the leaves. There was just a lovely smell of roses, and the animals waiting excitedly for the doors to open. Perfect!

The judge, Aunty the goat, went first. She looked very important. Then all the rest came in, one at a time. Last was Rambo, the big horse, who just poked in his head. Aunty was taken to the first display.

"So I just choose which flowers I like best?"
Aunty asked.

"Yes, we walk along the table, and whichever
display you think is best wins the prize. This is
Blink's display. She has
spent all morning getting
it right."

"It's called 'Daisies
and Dandelions',"
said Blink proudly.
The flowers were
white and yellow and
looked very pretty in a
bright blue mug. Aunty
looked at them carefully.
She sniffed them. And then she
ate them.

The others were so surprised, that they couldn't
speak! They just stared as Aunty went to the next
one, 'Buttercups and Roses'. She ate them too!

The goat tilted her head back, half closed her eyes in a very thoughtful sort of way, and compared 'Buttercups and Roses' with 'Daisies and Dandelions'.

Moving along the line, she ate 'Cowslips and Honeysuckle'. Then she ate 'Poppies and Krezanthasums... Crissansathums...

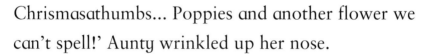

Chrismasathumbs... Poppies and another flower we can't spell!' Aunty wrinkled up her nose.

"Bit sour, that," she said. She turned at last and saw all the others looking at her with their mouths open. She looked from one to the other, red poppies drooping from the sides of her mouth.

"What?" she said, puzzled. "What!"

Rambo said gently, "You were supposed to judge how pretty the flowers are!"

Aunty was amazed.

"Flowers are pretty as well?" she asked.

Everyone burst out laughing. They had to explain it all to Aunty. She thought the whole idea of just looking at flowers was very odd.

There was no time to pick more flowers and start again. Instead, they gave Blink the prize...Aunty had decided that Blink's daisies and dandelions tasted the best!

At the end, the judge is always given a bunch of flowers as a small, 'thank you' gift. Aunty was so pleased...she ate it!

- Cuddly's -
JUMPER

Cuddly Sheep and Stout Pig were going to show the others how to knit. Cuddly Sheep was really good at knitting. But she needed her friend, Stout Pig, to help with the wool. Stout Pig couldn't knit, not even a little bit, but he was very good at spinning the wool for Cuddly to use.

Wool has to be made into yarn before you can knit with it. Yarn is made by twisting it, like string. That is what Stout did. He collected all the loose bits of wool that caught on thorny bushes around the farm and made long, beautiful lengths of yarn out of them. Then

Cuddly used Stout Pig's yarn to knit lots of pretty things. She could knit woolly socks. She could knit woolly hats. She could knit the best woolly jumpers in the world!

Cuddly and Stout sat close to each other. Stout Pig sat with his back against a low hedge and Cuddly sat on the other side. The pig pulled out lengths of wool from a pile under the hedge. He started to spin the wool on his wheel, until it was twisted into yarn and long enough to knit. Then he gave the end to Cuddly.

Cuddly made little loops of the wool and put them on two fat knitting needles. Then she started knitting.

"Knit one, purl one, knit two together," she whispered to herself. Only knitters know what these secret words mean. They must be magic words, because they are whispered over and over again.

"Knit one, purl one, knit two together."

The jumper quickly started to take shape. As it grew in size, the animals watching could see it was

the same colour as Cuddly's woolly coat, with little flecks in purple, like the berries on the hedge.

"Knit one, purl one, knit two together."

Stout had to work hard on the other side of the hedge to keep up with Cuddly Sheep.

"Knit one, purl one, knit two together…"

Cuddly looked up. "Is it getting late? I'm getting a bit cold," she said. None of the others felt cold.

"You can put my blanket on," said Pebbles the horse. He pulled his blanket over Cuddly's shoulders. But Cuddly got colder. And colder!

"I keep warm in the straw," said Saffron the cow. She covered Cuddly with straw. But the more Cuddly

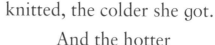

knitted, the colder she got. And the hotter Stout became. Cuddly was trying to finish the jumper quickly before she froze. The faster she knitted, the faster Stout Pig had to turn the spinning wheel, and he was soon in a sweat!

Then the jumper was finished…and Cuddly was shivering! Her teeth were chattering! Stout Pig flopped over the spinning wheel, trying to get his breath back. He was so hot and tired. Pebbles looked hard at Stout.

"Where did the wool come from that you were spinning?" he asked.

"I used that bundle of wool under the hedge," said Stout. "It was here when I came."

Pebbles' large head followed the wool from the spinning wheel over the hedge. There was only Cuddly there. "Cuddly," said Pebbles '...I think you have been knitting your own wool!"

Cuddly jumped up in surprise. The blanket and the straw fell off. She was bare all around her middle. No wonder she was cold. Her wool was all gone!

"Oh well," said Cuddly Sheep, taking out the needles from her knitting. "Never mind! I have a nice thick new jumper to keep me warm!"

— Clever —
BOOGIE

Boogie was a very clever pig. Most pigs aren't clever. They can't do sums. They can't tie their own shoelaces. Every single day they are given pig food to eat, and they say, "Oink! Oink! Pig food! My favourite!" They don't remember it's always the same.

But Boogie remembered every horrible meal he'd ever had, and was really fed up with pig food. It tasted like minced rubbish! Boogie lived in his own pen. It had a little shelter to keep the rain off,

and a small run to play in. In the field outside the
pigpen lived a sheep, a horse and a cow. There were
trees in the field too, but none near Boogie.

One day, acorns started falling from the biggest
tree. The tree was a long way from Boogie, but just a
few acorns bounced over and into his pen. Apples
began falling from another tree, and one rolled and
rolled, until it rolled into Boogie's pen.

Now, usually the only thing inside a pigpen is a
pig. They eat everything else! They eat the grass, the
roots, worms, stinging nettles, everything! All that is
left is a pig in mud! Pigs think anything else in a pen
must be food. So Boogie ate the acorns.

You probably know that acorns are really horrible to eat, but Boogie thought they were delicious! Then he ate the apple. He had never eaten anything so good in his life! He wanted all the acorns and apples! They were all around him, but he could not reach them. But he was a clever pig after all. Suddenly he had an idea.

Next to Boogie's pigpen was an old animal shed that had fallen to bits. Bricks and wood were spread about and wavy metal roof panels lay nearby.

Boogie said to the cow, "Will you move that metal roof for me? I'll give you some of my food if you do."

"I have all this grass to eat!" said the cow.

"But that's just plain grass," said Boogie. "This is pig food flavour in lumps!"

"Oh, all right!" said the cow. She pushed the roof under the apple tree.

"There! Is that in the right place?"

"Just move it forward…now turn it towards me… Good!"

Boogie gave the cow some of his pig food. The cow chewed for ages before she realised pig food did not have any actual taste in it. She spat it out.

"Pwah! Tastes like minced rubbish!" she said, and trotted off.

Boogie said to the horse, "Will you move that barrel for me? I'll give you some of my food if you do."

"I have all this grass to eat!" said the horse.

"But yours is green grass," said Boogie. "This is rich brown pig food in lumps!" So the horse moved the barrel where Boogie wanted it and was given the rest of the pig food.

"Yuck!" said the horse, when he tried it. "Do you really eat this rubbish?" And he galloped off too.

Boogie looked at the sheep. The sheep said, "I know – you want me to move something! I'll do it, but please don't give me any pig food!"

The sheep moved the drainpipe to where Boogie wanted it.

When the next apple fell, it rolled down the iron roof into the drainpipe and flew into Boogie's pen!

An acorn bounced off the barrel, and soon there were apples and acorns falling everywhere and bouncing into Boogie's pen.

Boogie dashed around, catching apples and acorns before they could even touch the ground!

And he never had to eat pig food again!

Lizzie and the
TRACTOR

Little Yellow the tractor came to a halt next to Lizzie the cow. The farmer leaned out of the tractor cab.

"Come on Lizzie, get up!" said the farmer. "We have the big farm show in one week. How are you going to win the 'Best Cow' prize if you laze around all day getting plump? You're so lazy!"

"I like lying here!" said Lizzie the cow. "I have all the grass I need right here next to me. I don't even have to get up!"

"You used to be the pride of the show, Lizzie!" wailed the farmer. "Wouldn't you like to be again?"

Lizzie munched on her mouthful and thought about it.

"No!" she said.

The farmer did not know what to do. All his animals won prizes except Lizzie. Perhaps they would know how to make Lizzie fit and lovely again.

He drove Little Yellow around the farm to ask their advice. Gorgeous the pig said, "She is too dull! Paint her pink with brown spots...it always works for me."

Reckless the goat said, "She eats too much grass. Get her to eat newspapers...it always works for me!"

Flash the cockerel said, "Her tail is too small. Stick lots of big bright feathers on her bottom…it always works for me!"

The farmer was disappointed. Those were silly ideas. Then Little Yellow said, "I can make Lizzie into the Best Cow again."

The animals snorted with laughter. How could a tractor do anything they could not? But the farmer just said, "Please do everything you can, Little Yellow!"

So Little Yellow bustled around in his barn, humming to himself and trying on all the bits and pieces that a tractor can make use of. First he put on his big bulldozer bucket and went over to Lizzie.

"Please Lizzie, move into the small field."

"Shan't!" said Lizzie, rolling onto her back.

So Little Yellow, to Lizzie's annoyance, scooped her up and took her into the field in the bucket. "It's for your own good," said Little Yellow.

Then Little Yellow put on his plough and, to everyone's amazement, ploughed up the grass in the middle of the field.

Next day, Little Yellow ploughed another strip in the middle of the field, and the day after that too. The ploughed bit was getting bigger and the grassy bit was getting smaller.

"Help!" cried Lizzie. "There is not enough grass left for me to eat! I'm getting thinner!"

Then tractor put on his grass cutter. He mowed all the grass that was left. If Lizzie lay down again she would not get enough to eat.

She had to work hard just to find enough grass. She was smaller now, and the exercise was making her coat glossy.

But the tractor was not finished. He put on his back forks and took Lizzie a bale of hay to eat, but as she rushed to eat it, he drove away, and she had to trot

behind to keep up. By the end of the day she was very tired, but fit and healthy too.

By this time, Little Yellow had used nearly every tool he had! The last thing he used was a power spray to wash her down, and…Ta-ra! There stood Lizzie, more beautiful than ever before!

Lizzie went to the show, and of course was declared 'Best Cow'. She had a lovely blue ribbon hung around her neck and the farmer was given a silver cup. All thanks to Little Yellow the tractor!

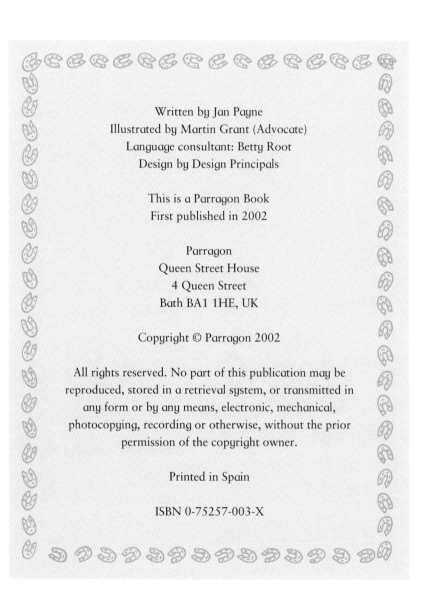

Written by Jan Payne
Illustrated by Martin Grant (Advocate)
Language consultant: Betty Root
Design by Design Principals

This is a Parragon Book
First published in 2002

Parragon
Queen Street House
4 Queen Street
Bath BA1 1HE, UK

Printed in Spain

ISBN 0-75257-003-X

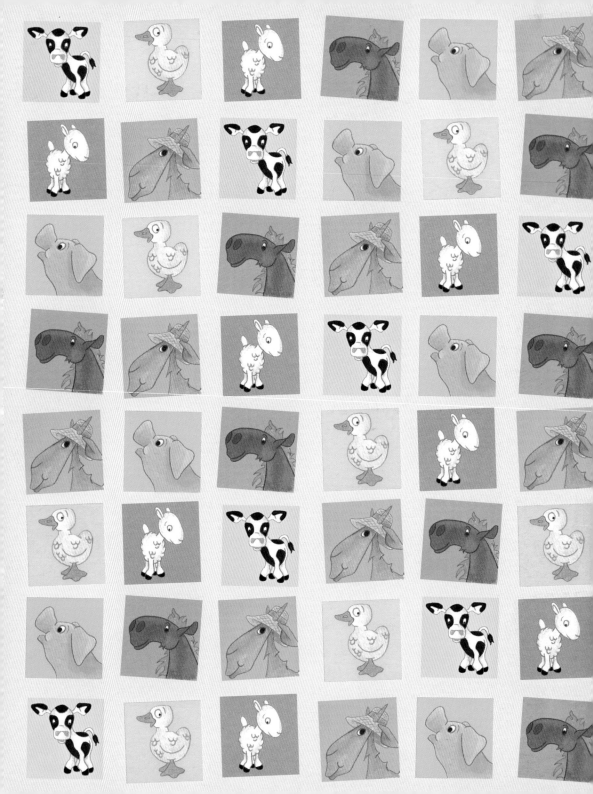